Art Nouveau Designs

All rights reserved.
Copyright © 2007 Pepin van Roojen

The Pepin Press / Agile Rabbit editions
P.O. Box 10349
1001 EH Amsterdam, The Netherlands

Tel +31 20 4202021
Fax +31 20 4201152
mail@pepinpress.com
www.pepinpress.com

ISBN 978 90 5768 013 7

Concept & series editor: Pepin van Roojen
Layout for this volume: Joost Hölscher
Cover Design: Pepin van Roojen

10 9 8
2007

Manufactured in Singapore

The Pepin Press – Agile Rabbit Editions

Graphic Themes
978-90-5768-062-5   Fancy Alphabets
978-90-5768-055-7   Signs & Symbols
978-90-5768-016-8   Graphic Ornaments (2 CDs)

Textile Patterns
978-90-5768-100-4   Kimono Patterns
978-90-5768-004-5   Batik Patterns
978-90-5768-030-4   Weaving Patterns

Pattern & Design Collections
978-90-5768-005-2   Floral Patterns
978-90-5768-107-3   Marble Paper Design

Styles (Cultural)
978-90-5768-071-7   Arabian Geometric Patterns
978-90-5768-022-9   Traditional Dutch Tile Designs
978-90-5768-073-1   Barcelona Tile Designs

Styles (Historical)
978-90-5768-097-7   Jugendstil
978-90-5768-072-4   Art Deco
978-90-5768-060-1   Fancy Designs 1920

Photographs
987-90-5768-047-2   Fruit
978-90-5768-048-9   Vegetables
978-90-5768-070-0   Flowers

Folding & Packaging
978-90-5768-039-7   How To Fold
978-90-5768-044-1   Structural Package Designs

Web Design
978-90-5768-105-9   Web Design Index 7
978-90-5768-103-5   Web Design Ind. by Content2

Picture Collections
978-90-5768-052-6   Astrology
978-90-5768-066-3   Mythology Pictures
978-90-5768-051-9   Historical & Curious Maps

More titles in preparation.
In addition to the Agile Rabbit series of book +CD-ROM sets,
The Pepin Press publishes a wide range of books on art, design,
architecture, applied art, and popular culture.

Please visit www.pepinpress.com for more information.

Contents

Free CD-Rom in the inside back cover

English

This book contains images for use as a graphic resource, or inspiration. All the illustrations are stored in high-resolution format on the enclosed free CD-ROM (Mac and Windows) and are ready to use for professional quality printed media and web page design. The pictures can also be used to produce postcards, either on paper or digitally, or to decorate your letters, flyers, etc.

They can be imported directly from the CD into most design, image-manipulation, illustration, word-processing and e-mail programs; no installation is required. Some programs will allow you to access the images directly; in others, you will first have to create a document, and then import the images. Please consult your software manual for instructions.

The names of the files on the CD-ROM correspond with the page numbers in this book. For pages with more than one image, the order is from left to right and from top to bottom. This is indicated with a number following the page number, or with the following letter codes: T = top, B = bottom, C = centre, L = left, and R = right.

The CD-ROM comes free with this book, but is not for sale separately. The publishers do not accept any responsibility should the CD not be compatible with your system.

For non-professional applications, single images can be used free of charge. The images cannot be used for any type of commercial or otherwise professional application – including all types of printed or digital publications – without prior permission from The Pepin Press/Agile Rabbit Editions.

For inquiries about permissions and fees:
mail@pepinpress.com
Fax +31 20 4201152

Español

En este libro podrá encontrar imágenes que le servirán como fuente de material gráfico o como inspiración para realizar sus propios diseños. Se adjunta un CD-ROM gratuito (Mac y Windows) donde hallará todas las ilustraciones en un formato de alta resolución, con las que podrá conseguir una impresión de calidad profesional y diseñar páginas web. Las imágenes pueden también emplearse para realizar postales, de papel o digitales, o para decorar cartas, folletos, etc.

Estas imágenes se pueden importar desde el CD a la mayoría de programas de diseño, manipulación de imágenes, dibujo, tratamiento de textos y correo electrónico, sin necesidad de utilizar un programa de instalación. Algunos programas le permitirán acceder a las imágenes directamente; otros, sin embargo, requieren la creación previa de un documento para importar las imágenes. Consulte su manual de software en caso de duda.

Los nombres de los archivos del CD-ROM se corresponden con los números de página de este libro. En aquellas páginas en las que haya más de una imagen, el orden que se ha de seguir para localizarlas es de izquierda a derecha y de arriba abajo. Esto se indica con un número a continuación del número de página, o con las siguientes abreviaturas: T (top)= arriba; B (bottom)= abajo; C (centre)= centro; L (left)= izquierda y R (right)= derecha.

El CD-ROM se ofrece de manera gratuita con este libro, pero está prohibida su venta por separado. Los editores no asumen ninguna responsabilidad en el caso de que el CD no sea compatible con su sistema.

Se autoriza el uso de estas imágenes de manera gratuita para aplicaciones no profesionales. No se podrán emplear en aplicaciones de tipo profesional o comercial (incluido cualquier tipo de publicación impresa o digital) sin la autorización previa de The Pepin Press/Agile Rabbit Editions.

Para más información acerca de autorizaciones y tarifas:
mail@pepinpress.com
Fax +31 20 4201152

Português

Este livro contém imagens que podem ser utilizadas como fonte de material gráfico ou como inspiração para realizar os seus próprios desenhos. Você encontrará todas as ilustrações em formato de alta resolução dentro do CD–ROM gratuito (Mac e Windows), e com elas poderá conseguir uma impressão de qualidade profissional e desenhar páginas web. As imagens também podem ser usadas para criar postais, de papel ou digitais, ou para decorar cartas, folhetos, etc.

Estas imagens podem ser importadas do CD para a maioria de programas de desenho, manipulação de imagem, ilustração, processamento de texto e correio eletrônico, sem a necessidade de utilizar um programa de instalação. Alguns programas permitirão que você tenha acesso às imagens diretamente; e em outros, você deverá criar um documento antes de importar as imagens. Por favor, consulte o seu manual de software para obter maiores informações.

Os nomes dos arquivos do CD–ROM correspondem aos números de página deste livro. Nas páginas onde exista mais de uma imagem, a ordem que deve ser seguida para localizar as imagens é da esquerda para a direita e de cima para baixo. Isso é indicado com um número que vem logo depois do número de página, ou com as seguintes abreviaturas: T (*top*)= acima; B (*bottom*)= abaixo; C (*centre*)= centro; L (*left*)= esquerda e R (*right*)= direita.

O CD–ROM é oferecido de forma gratuita com este livro, porém é proibido vendê-lo separadamente. Os editores não assumem nenhuma responsabilidade no caso de que o CD não seja compatível com o seu sistema.

Desde que não seja para aplicação profissional, as imagens individuais podem ser utilizadas gratuitamente.

As imagens não podem ser empregadas em nenhum tipo de aplicação comercial ou profissional - incluindo todos os tipos de publicações impressas ou digitais - sem a prévia permissão de The Pepin Press/Agile Rabbit Editions.

Para esclarecer dúvidas a respeito das permissões e taxas:
mail@pepinpress.com
Fax +31 20 4201152

Français

Cet ouvrage renferme des illustrations destinées à servir de ressources graphiques ou d'inspiration. La totalité des images sont stockées en format haute définition sur le CD-ROM gratuit inclus (Mac et Windows), prêtes à l'emploi en vue de réaliser des impressions ou pages Web de qualité professionnelle. Elles permettent également de créer des cartes postales, aussi bien sur papier que virtuelles, ou d'agrémenter vos courriers, prospectus et autres.

Vous pouvez les importer directement à partir du CD dans la plupart des applications de création, manipulation graphique, illustration, traitement de texte et messagerie, sans qu'aucune installation ne soit nécessaire. Certaines applications permettent d'accéder directement aux images, tandis que dans d'autres, vous devez d'abord créer un document, puis importer les images. Veuillez consultez les instructions dans le manuel du logiciel concerné.

Sur le CD, les noms des fichiers correspondent aux numéros de pages de ce livre. Sur les pages qui comportent plusieurs images, l'ordre va de gauche à droite, et de haut en bas. Il est indiqué soit par un numéro figurant après le numéro de page, soit par les codes suivants : T (top)= haut, B (bottom)= bas, C (centre)= centre, L (left)= gauche, et R (right)= droite.

Le CD-ROM est fourni gratuitement avec le livre, mais il ne peut être vendu séparément. L'éditeur décline toute responsabilité si ce CD n'est pas compatible avec votre ordinateur.

Vous pouvez utiliser les images individuelles sans frais dans des applications non-professionnelles. Il est interdit d'utiliser les images avec des applications de type professionnel ou commercial (y compris toutes les sortes de publications numériques ou imprimés) sans l'autorisation préalable de The Pepin Press/Agile Rabbit Editions.

Pour tout renseignement relatif aux autorisations et aux frais d'utilisation:
mail@pepinpress.com
Fax +31 20 4201152

Italiano

Questo libro contiene immagini che possono essere utilizzate come risorsa grafica o come fonte di ispi-razione. Tutte le illustrazioni sono contenute nell'allegato CD–ROM gratuito (per Mac e Windows), in for-mato ad alta risoluzione e pronte per essere utilizzate per pubblicazioni professionali e pagine web.
Possono essere inoltre usate per creare cartoline, su carta o digitali, o per abbellire lettere, opuscoli, ecc.
Dal CD, le immagini possono essere importate direttamente nella maggior parte dei programmi di grafica, di ritocco, di illustrazione, di scrittura e di posta elettronica; non è richiesto alcun tipo di installazione.
Alcuni programmi vi consentiranno di accedere alle immagini direttamente; in altri, invece, dovrete prima creare un documento e poi importare le immagini. Consultate il manuale del software per maggiori infor-mazioni.
I nomi dei documenti sul CD–ROM corrispondono ai numeri delle pagine del libro. Quando le pagine con-tengono più di un'immagine, l'ordine di queste ultime è da sinistra a destra e dall'alto verso il basso.
L'ordine è indicato con un numero situato dopo il numero di pagina o con le seguenti lettere: T (*top*)= alto, B (*bottom*)= basso, C (*centre*)= centro, L (*left*)= sinistra e R (*right*)= destra.
Il CD–ROM è allegato gratuitamente al libro e non può essere venduto separatamente. L'editore non può essere ritenuto responsabile qualora il CD non fosse compatibile con il sistema posseduto.
Per applicazioni di tipo non professionale, le singole immagini possono essere utilizzate gratuitamente. Se desiderate, invece, utilizzare le immagini per applicazioni di tipo professionale o con scopi commerciali, comprese tutte le pubblicazioni digitali o stampate, sarà necessaria la relativa autorizzazione da parte della casa editrice The Pepin Press/Agile Rabbit Editions.

Per ulteriori informazioni su autorizzazioni e canoni per il diritto di sfruttamento commerciale rivolgetevi a:
mail@pepinpress.com
Fax +31 20 4201152

Deutsch

Dieses Buch enthält Bilder, die als Ausgangsmaterial für graphische Zwecke oder als Anregung genutzt werden können. Alle Abbildungen sind in hoher Auflösung auf der beiliegenden Gratis-CD–ROM (für Mac und Windows) gespeichert und lassen sich direkt zum Drucken in professioneller Qualität oder zur Gestaltung von Websites einsetzen. Sie können sie auch als Motive für Postkarten auf Karton oder in digitaler Form, oder als Ausschmückung für Ihre Briefe, Flyer etc. verwenden.

Die Bilder lassen sich direkt in die meisten Zeichen-, Bildbearbeitungs-, Illustrations-, Textverarbeitungs- und E-Mail-Programme laden, ohne dass zusätzliche Programme installiert werden müssen. In einigen Programmen können die Dokumente direkt geladen werden, in anderen müssen Sie zuerst ein Dokument anlegen und können dann die Datei importieren. Genauere Hinweise dazu finden Sie im Handbuch zu Ihrer Software.

Die Namen der Bilddateien auf der CD–ROM entsprechen den Seitenzahlen dieses Buchs. Bei Seiten mit mehreren Bildern verläuft die Reihenfolge von links nach rechts und oben nach unten. Wo die Position auf der jeweiligen Seite angegeben ist, bedeutet T (top)= oben, B (bottom)= unten, C (centre)= Mitte, L (left)= links und R (right)= rechts.

Die CD–ROM wird kostenlos mit dem Buch geliefert und ist nicht separat verkäuflich. Der Verlag haftet nicht für Inkompatibilität der CD–ROM mit Ihrem System.

Für nicht professionelle Anwendungen können einzelne Bilder kostenfrei genutzt werden. Die Bilder dürfen ohne vorherige Genehmigung von The Pepin Press /Agile Rabbit Editions nicht für kommerzielle oder sonstige professionelle Anwendungen einschließlich aller Arten von gedruckten oder digitalen Medien eingesetzt werden.

Für Fragen zu Genehmigungen und Preisen wenden Sie sich bitte an:
mail@pepinpress.com
Fax +31 20 4201152

日本語

本書にはグラフィック リソースやインスピレーションとして使用できる美しいイメージ画像が含まれています。すべてのイラストレーションは、無料の付属 CD-ROM（Mac および Windows 用）に高解像度で保存されており、これらを利用してプロ品質の印刷物や WEB ページを簡単に作成することができます。また、紙ベースまたはデジタルの葉書の作成やレター、ちらしの装飾等に使用することもできます。

これらの画像は、CD から主なデザイン、画像処理、イラスト、ワープロ、E メールソフトウェアに直接取り込むことができます。インストレーションは必要ありません。プログラムによっては、画像に直接アクセスできる場合や、一旦ドキュメントを作成した後に画像を取り込む場合等があります。詳細は、ご使用のソフトウェアのマニュアルをご参照下さい。

CD-ROM 上のファイル名は、本書のページ数に対応しています。ページに複数の画像が含まれる場合は、左から右、上から下の順番で番号がつけられ、ページ番号に続く数字または下記のレターコードで識別されます。

T ＝トップ（上部）、B＝ボトム（下部）、C ＝センター（中央）、L＝レフト（左）R ＝ライト（右）

CD-ROM は本書の付属品であり、別売されておりません。CD がお客様のシステムと互換でなかった場合、発行者は責任を負わないことをご了承下さい。

プロ用以外のアプリケーションで、画像を一回のみ無料で使用することができます。The Pepin Press / Agile Rabbit Editions から事前許可を得ることなく、あらゆる形体の印刷物、デジタル出版物をはじめとする、あらゆる種類の商業用ならびにプロ用アプリケーションで画像を使用することを禁止します。

使用許可と料金については、下記までお問い合わせ下さい。

mail@pepinpress.com

ファックス： +31 20 4201152

中 文

本書包含精美圖片，可以作為圖片資源或激發靈感的資料使用。這些圖片存儲在所附的高清晰度免費 CD-ROM (可在 Mac 和 Windows 下使用) 中，可用於專業的高品質印刷媒體和網頁設計。圖片還可以用於製作紙質和數字明信片，或裝飾您的信封、傳單等。您無需安裝即可以把圖片直接從 CD 調入大多數的設計、圖像處理、圖片、文字處理和電子郵件程序。有些程序允許您直接使用圖片；另外一些，您則需要先創建一個文件，然後引入圖片。用法說明請參閱軟體說明書。

在 CD 中的文件名稱是與書中的頁碼相對應的。如果書頁中的圖片超過一幅，其順序為從左到右，從上到下。這會在書頁號後加一個數字來表示，或者是加一個字母： T = 上， B = 下，

C = 中， L = 左， R = 右。

本書附帶的 CD-ROM 是免費的，但 CD-ROM 不單獨出售。如果 CD 與您的系統不相容，出版商不承擔任何責任。

就非專業的用途而言，可以免費使用單個圖片。若未事先得到 The Pepin Press/Agile Rabbit Editions 的許可，不得將圖片用於任何其他類型的商業或專業用途 - 包括所有類型的印刷或數字出版物。

有關許可及收費的詢問，請查詢：

Mail@pepinpress.com

傳真： +31 20 4201152

Die SECESSION

CHAMPAGNE

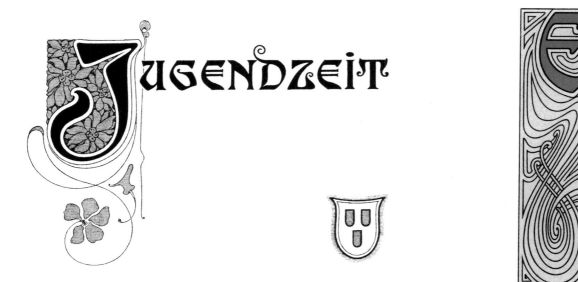

JUGENDZEIT

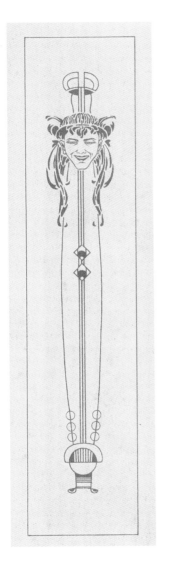

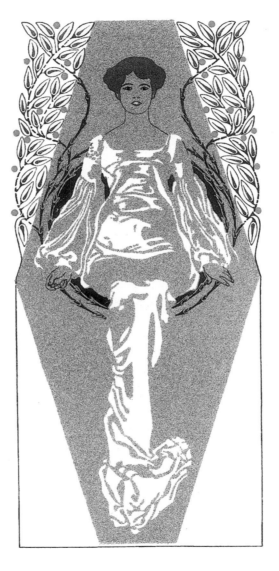

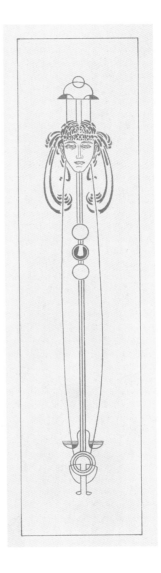

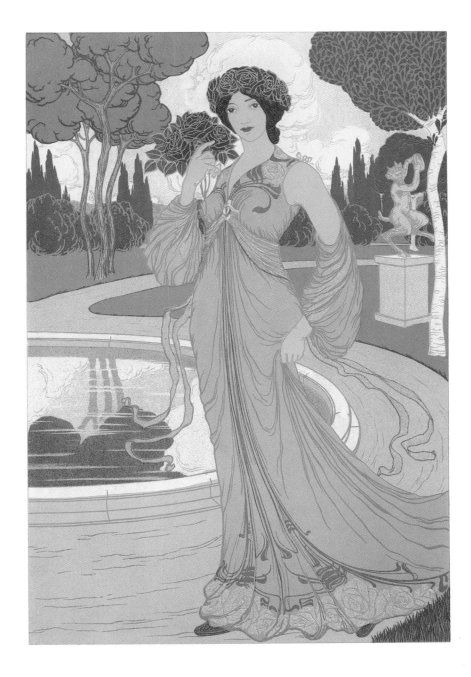

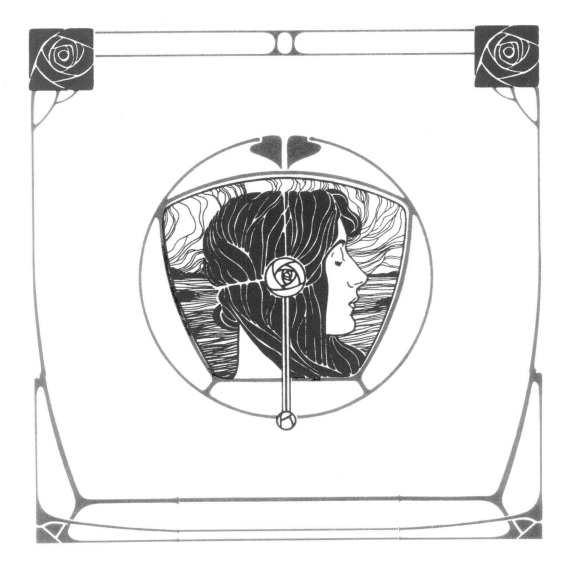

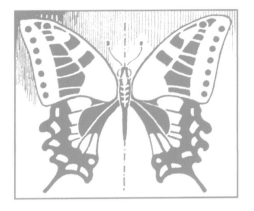

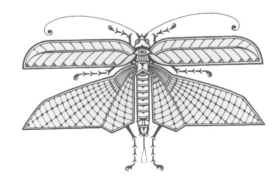

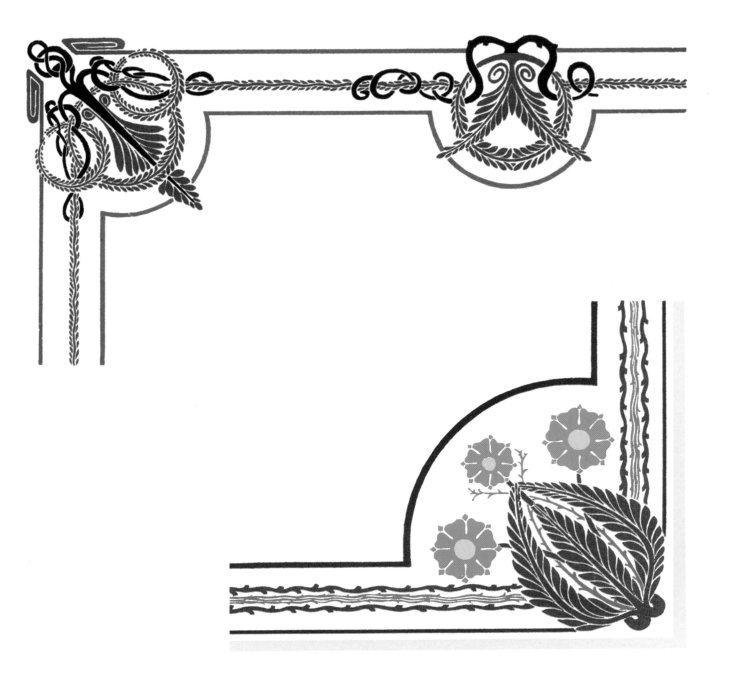

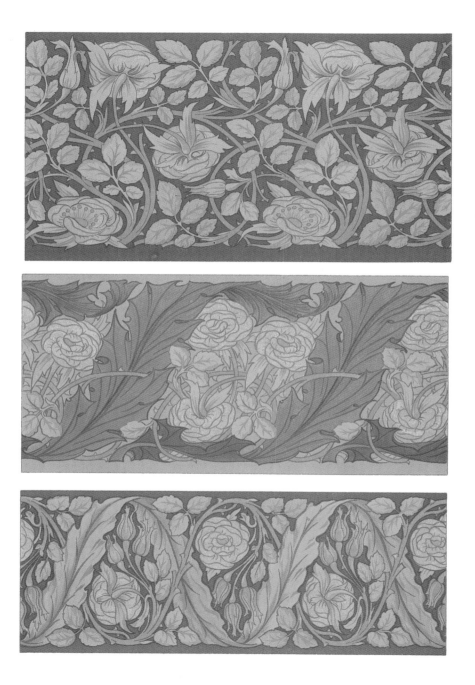

59

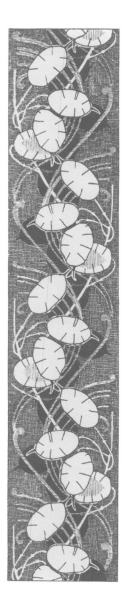

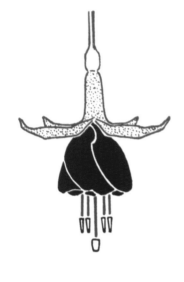

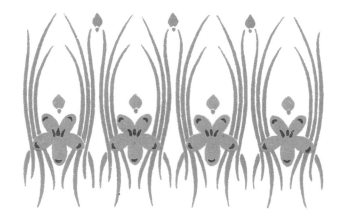

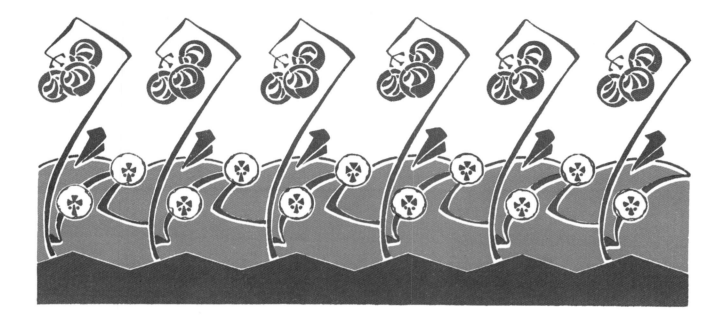

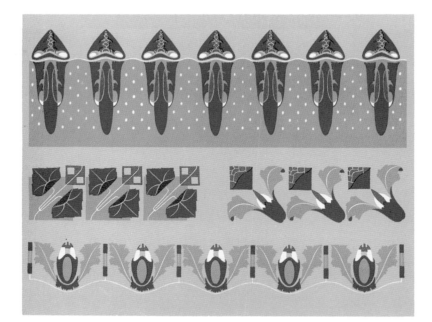

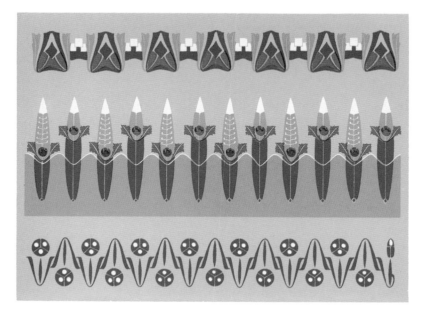

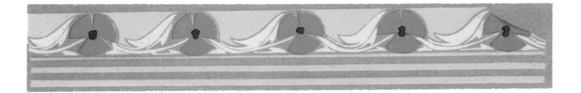

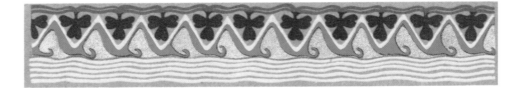

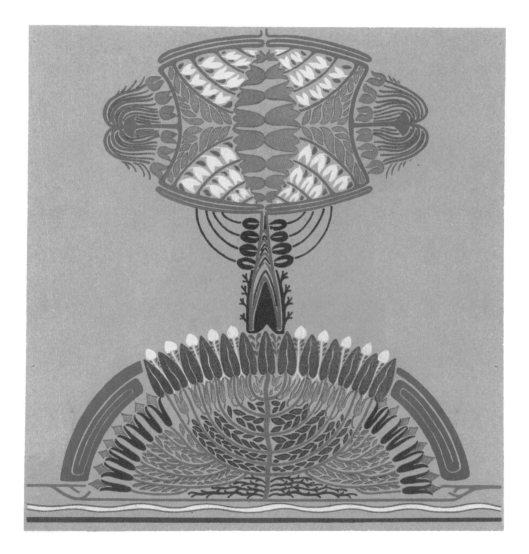

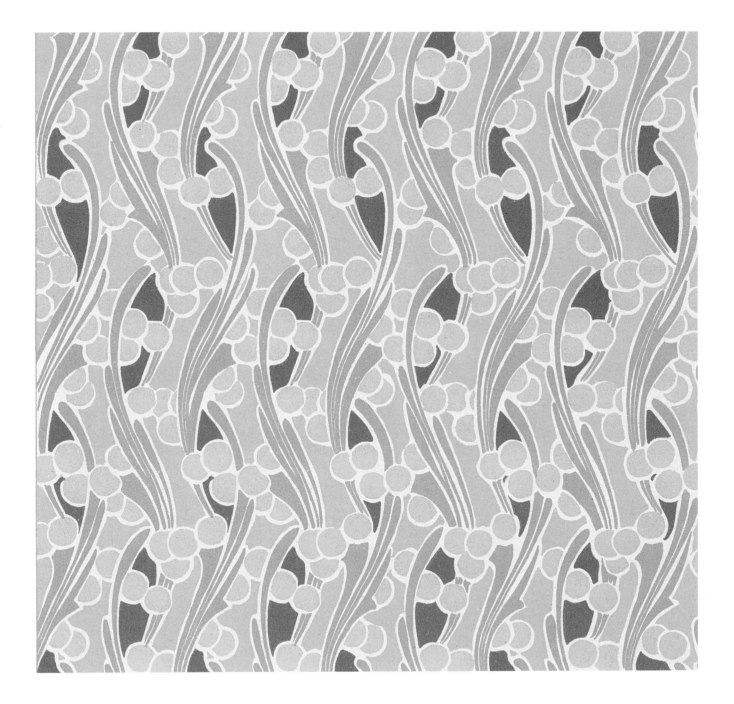

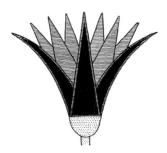

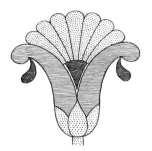

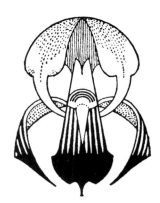

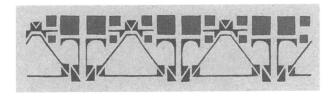

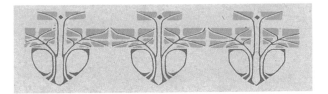

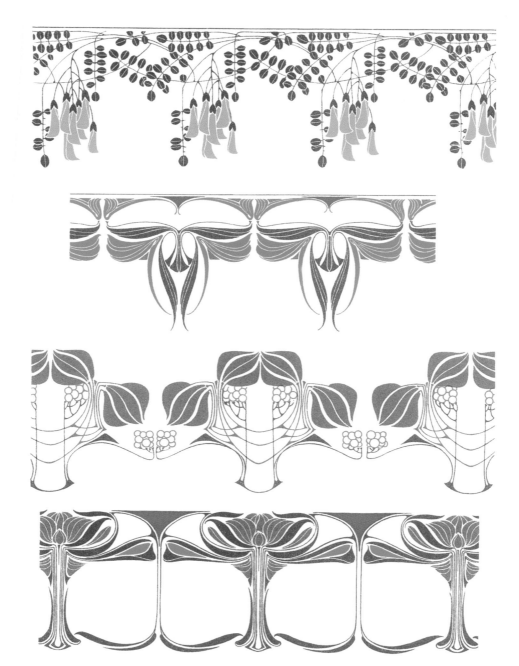

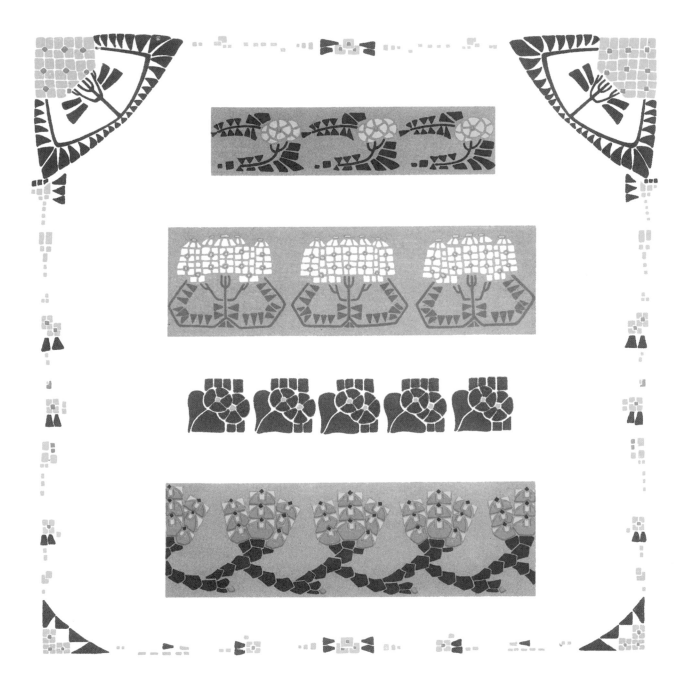

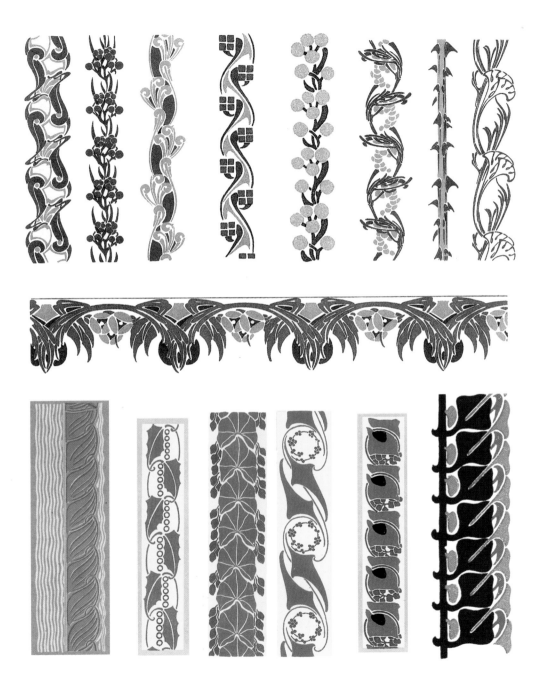

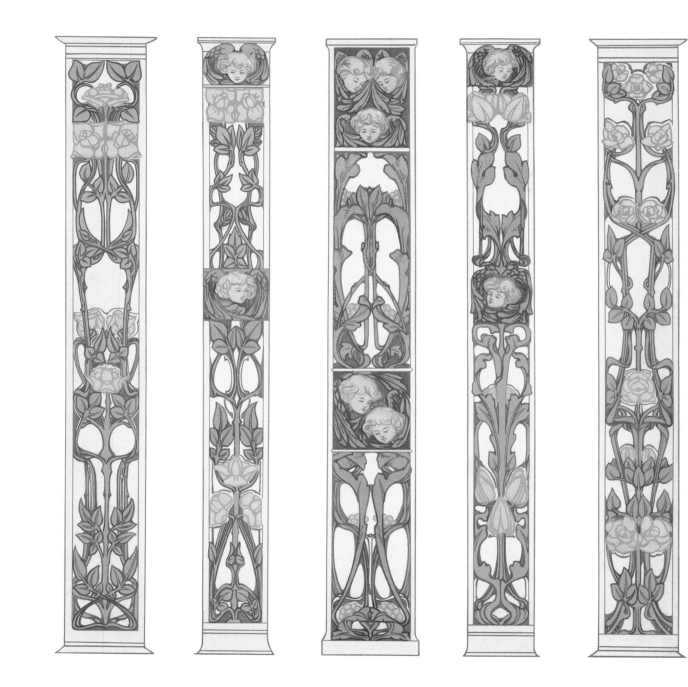

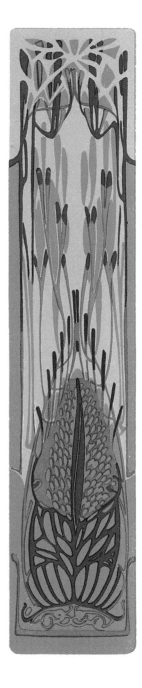

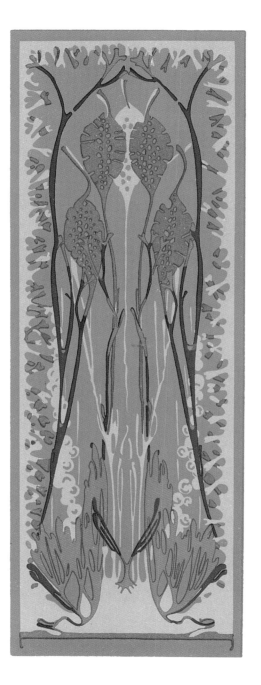

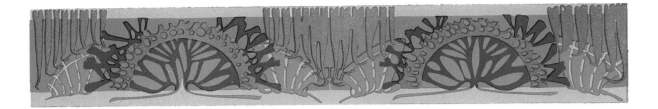

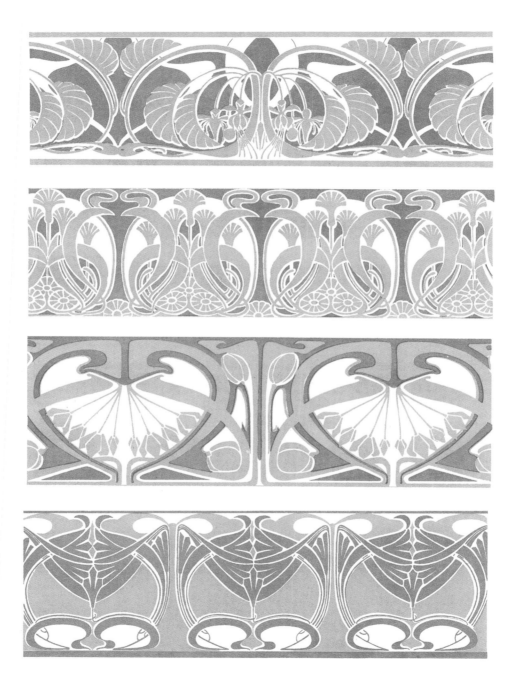

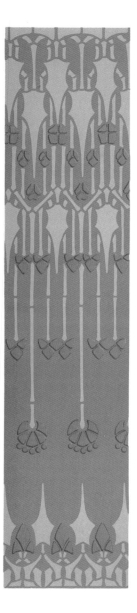
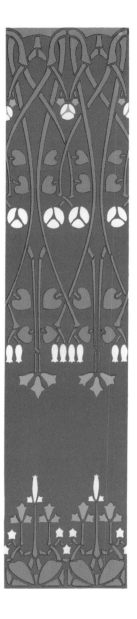

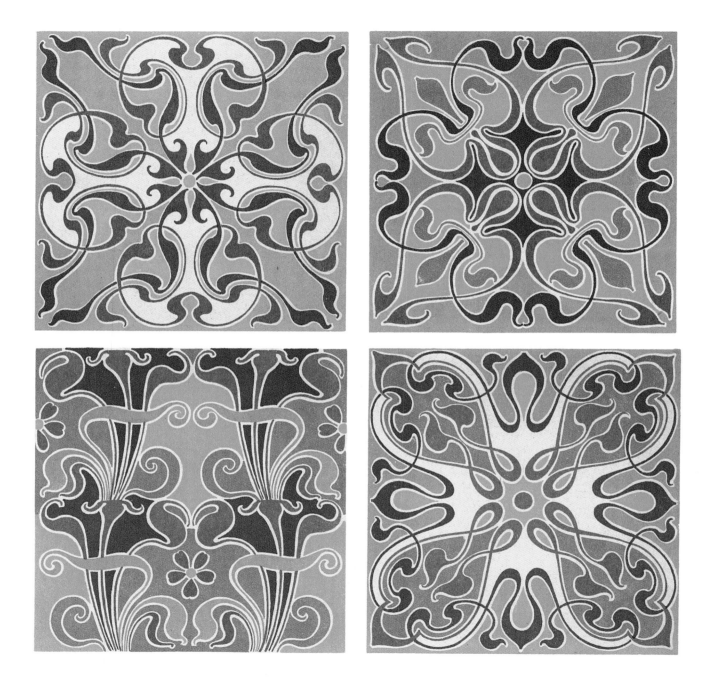

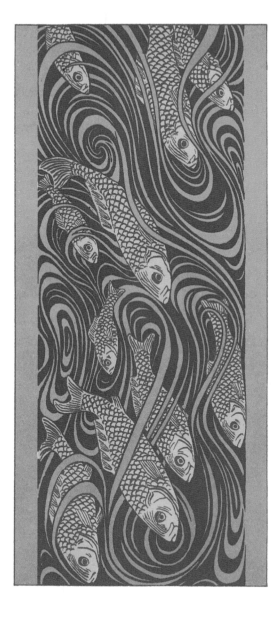

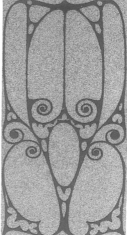

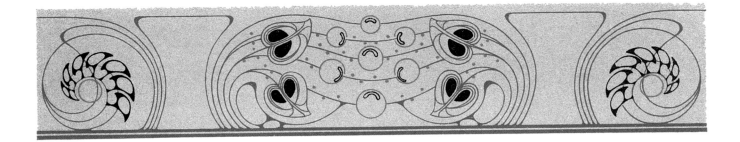

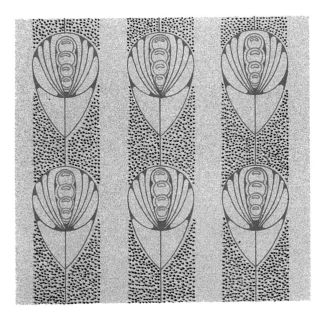

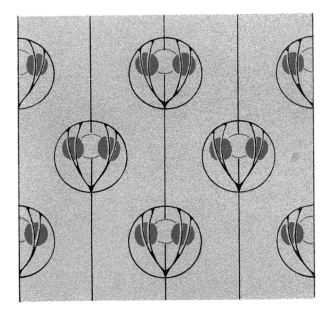

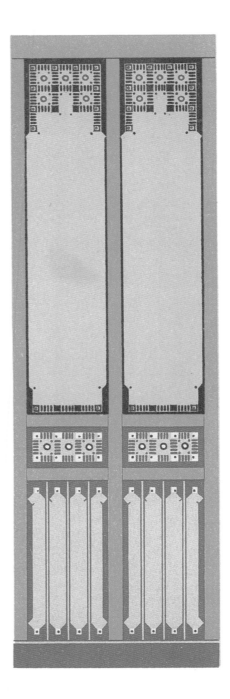

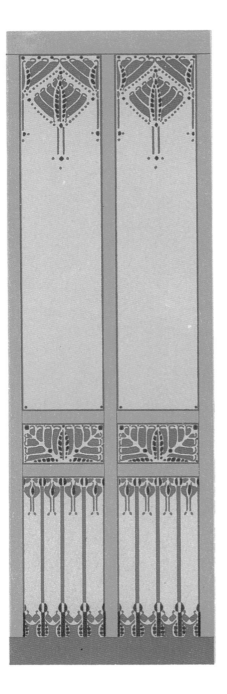

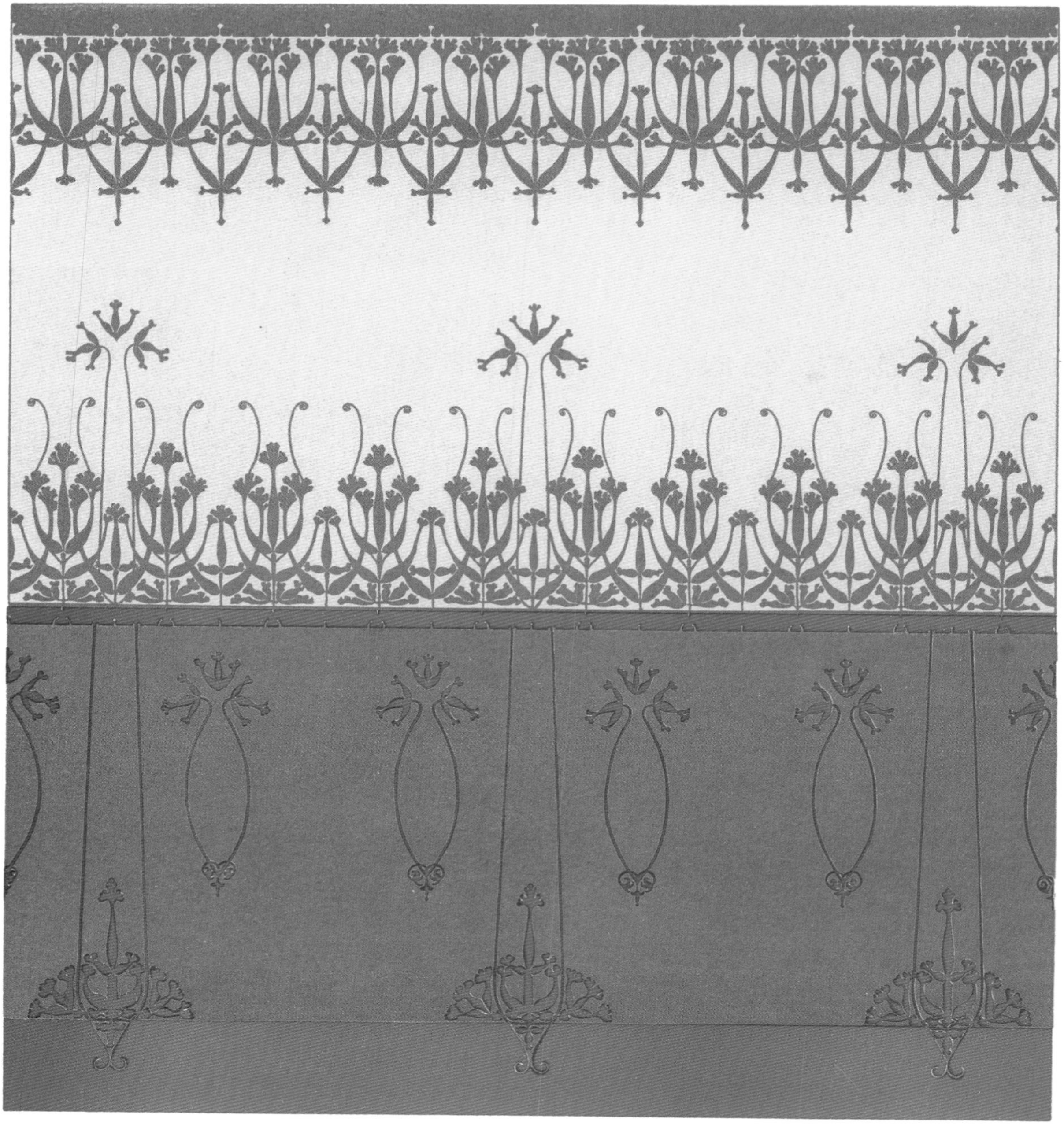

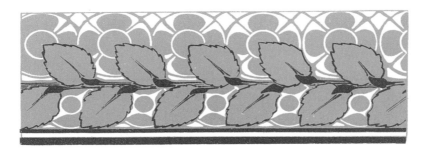

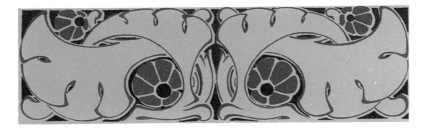

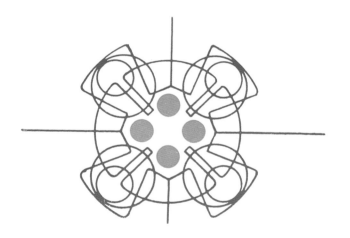

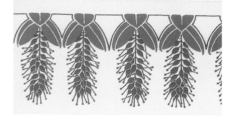

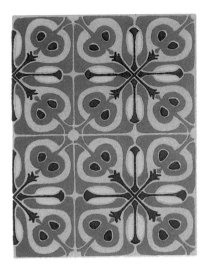
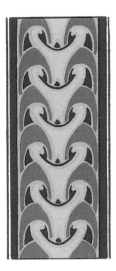

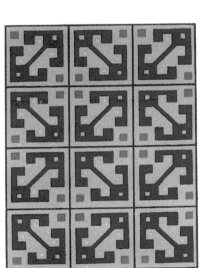

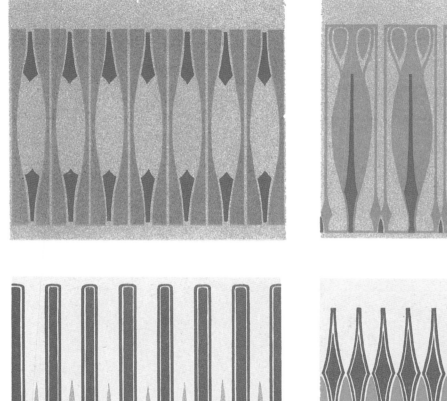

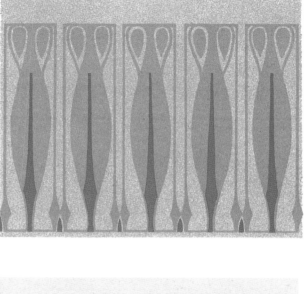

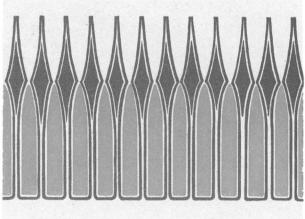

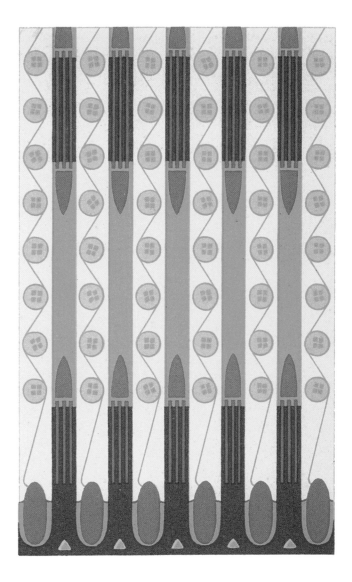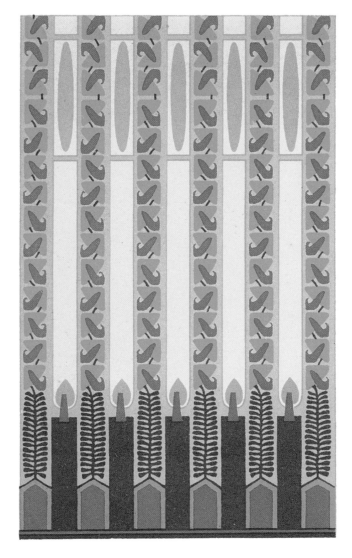

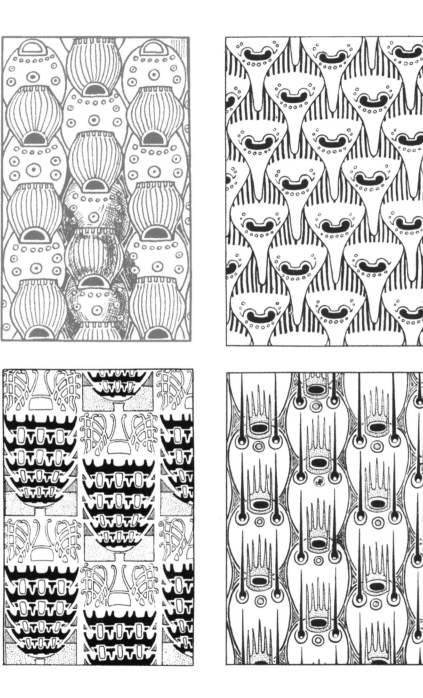

126

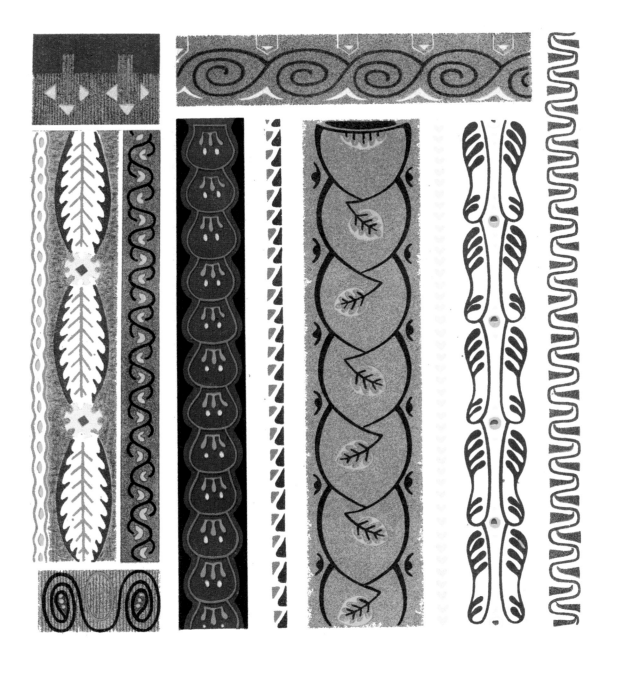

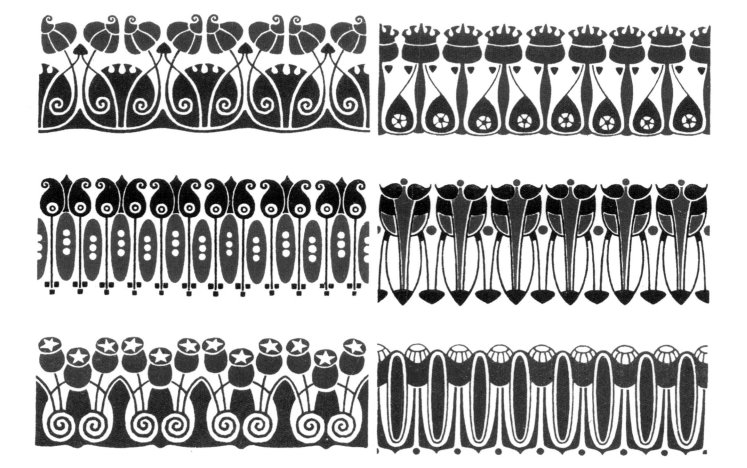

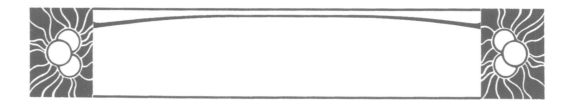

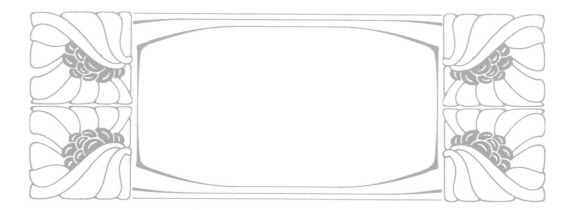

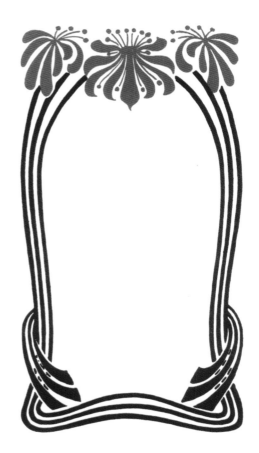

136

138

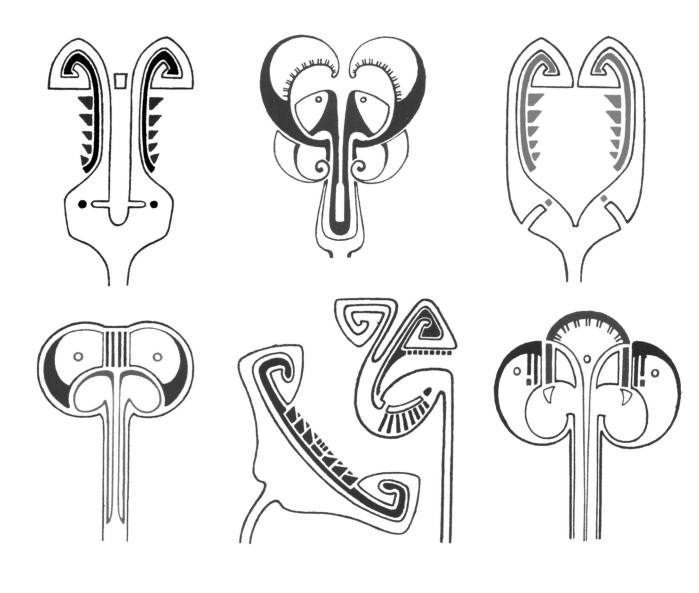

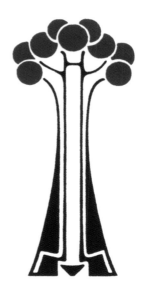

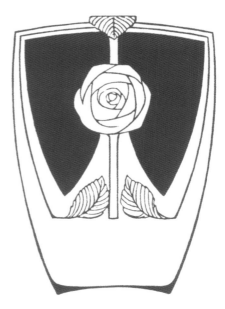

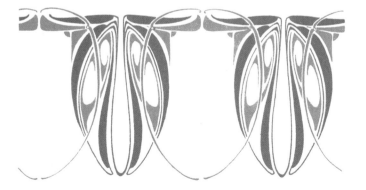